Seven Steps to Leading a Gender Balanced Business

AVIVAH WITTENBERG–COX

20-first Publishing, London UK

All cartoons are courtesy Roger Beale.

The web addresses in this book were correct at the time of the book's publication but may be subject to change.

CONTENTS

FOREWORD – Marijn Dekkers, CEO Bayer

As a research-based company, Bayer usually sees innovation through the lens of scientific or technical breakthroughs. Yet the company's approach to leadership can also be considered innovative.

For the past two years, based on the advice that appears in *Seven Steps to Leading a Gender balanced Business*, Bayer has been quietly building awareness and skills to lead across cultures and genders across all its global teams. Many of our corporate neighbours are responding to the legal and political pressures of European gender quotas by implementing initiatives focused on women.

I share Avivah Wittenberg-Cox's idea that it's time for companies to take a much broader look at the realities of changing markets and the demographics of talent. The globalization of markets and the dramatic increase in the number of women among the world's educated workforce are drivers for any multinational company interested in growth and innovative responses to fast-changing conditions.

Many of Bayer's senior leadership teams worldwide have held the kind of strategic debates described in this book. They focused on *why* and *how* we want to adjust the balance of national cultures and genders in the company's management. Division heads, country managers and functional teams have used these sessions to analyse and understand shifting global and national trends and statistics in both talent and markets – and craft action plans to adapt mind-sets, processes and plans.

This book offers clear guidelines on how to create sustainable gender and cultural balance. Notably, that initiatives should be *leader-led, strategically focused* and *business-driven. Accountability for change must lie with leaders* to define and implement the balance that makes the most sense to their changing business realities. And CEOs must recognize that it takes time to build awareness and skills for managers to effectively lead across cultures and genders.

Based on a recently completed survey of a cross section of the organization's leaders, senior management at Bayer is now aligned on the need for change. There is also a widespread recognition that this is the responsibility of leaders and managers – not HR or diversity departments. This investment should now accelerate the already-improving balance we are seeing in management.

This is the beginning of a journey. Bayer's talent pipeline, the profile of our senior executives and the company's management composition have all steadily evolved over the past two years. The goal is not to change overnight. Instead, we are committed to making steady progress in reflecting the markets we serve and the talent we have internally. I am personally committed to this objective, and I recognize that leadership is the key to unlocking the benefits that better balance will bring to Bayer. This book shows the way, but the buck stops with every CEO.

PART 1

Recognize the Business Opportunity

1. Reframe the Debate

Ask a roomful of men what the most significant event of the twentieth century was and you'll hear about man's magnificent first steps on the moon. Ask a roomful of women and you'll hear it's the invention of the pill. History is inevitably shaped by the language and lens through which it's seen. So, this book will argue, is your future.

We are at an exciting, unprecedented moment in human history. The twentieth century saw the rise of women, a change that universally transformed life as we know it. The shift to a more equal balance of power between men and women is resulting in one of humanity's most profound revolutions. The consequences are political, demographic, social, cultural and – critically – economic.

The business world has not yet fully embraced the consequences or the potential that this new gender balance offers. So competitive edge lies in first-mover advantage: In the twenty-first century, companies that get it right and leverage the potential of women as both talent and market will profit massively by the huge numbers at play. IBM, General Motors and Lockheed Martin are all companies that have recently appointed their first female CEOs. They are trying to tap into innovation, new leadership styles and improved relationships with evolving customer bases.

Economic crises and crises of leadership are calling for new ways of seeing–and running–economies and companies. 20-first is one of the world's leading gender consultancies. Over the past decade, we have worked with many of the world's leading multinational companies, in almost every sector, and in nearly every country. All of our clients are working on developing new and more balanced leadership styles, more customer centricity, more understanding of growth market subtleties and more innovation. Some business leaders recognize the transformational opportunities that can be unleashed by a strategic management of gender. For some, it is a key lever to achieve strategic objectives. Others still don't even see it as business relevant. Most of today's Western managers have been taught that equality between the sexes means eliminating differences – of opportunity, treatment, salary and so on. But to take full advantage of the specific strengths women can bring to a company, leaders must understand and maximize the complementary differences between men and women. Managers who are effectively able to harness these differences will be the ones to grow, innovate and excel in the twenty-first century. In addition to the ethical discourses around equality that have powered the staggering changes of the past decades, the new global reality makes gender balance one of the biggest – and I will argue one of the easiest – ways to make companies grow, innovate and excel sustainably.

This will require a change of frame and vocabulary. Let me start by defining some key terms: "gender bilingualism" and "gender balance." They are key to building the organizations of the future.

"Gender bilingual" organizations and managers have developed the management competencies to understand the differences between men and women so that they are able to effectively understand, connect and communicate with 100 percent of potential customers, end-users and stakeholders. They are also skilled at being able to attract, retain and develop 100 percent of the available talent pool. Consider: when companies invest in China, Russia, or Brazil, they know they need to learn the language and culture of the market they are targeting. In a century where women have become the dominant talent pool and the dominant market makers, why aren't more companies eager to learn the language and culture of women and how it differs from those of men?

"Gender balance" does not necessarily mean numerical equality. Instead, it means a conscious analysis of the gender mix that reflects the available talent pool and sustainably supports strategic goals. It recognizes that gender matters as a lever for business performance, that 60 percent of global university graduates are now women, and that under-utilizing the majority of the talent is not a good guarantee of future success. As one CEO told me, the goal does "not necessarily have to be 50/50 but should be closer to 50/50 than to 85/15."

This book is written for progressive leaders who are interested in harnessing the rise of educated, empowered women in the workforce – as well as in the consumer market. I have had the pleasure of working with many such forward-thinking leaders; this book is a tribute to their inspirational work.

Throughout this book, you'll see "Frontline Feedback" boxes, which feature real reactions to gender issues from leaders I've worked with. Many companies don't feel comfortable openly discussing their ratio of men to women, or the challenges and rewards of becoming a gender balanced organization. But industry-leading firms are quietly making progress in realizing this opportunity – and you can, too.

FRONTLINE FEEDBACK: *"The way the topic has now been positioned helped the team see that it isn't a problem or a fight for numbers/KPI results. It helped everyone see that this is a way of creating value for the company. It freed up peoples' minds."*

Simplify the Business Case

Today 59 percent of global university graduates are female, according to the OECD.[1] Women's educational empowerment, combined with a shift from manufacturing-dominated twentieth-century economies to services-dominated twenty-first-century economies has led to economic independence, rising incomes and a narrowing gender gap in global labour forces. Women also represent most of the consumer market. In fact, 80 percent of consumer goods purchasing decisions are in the hands of women. Increasingly, women make the majority of buying decisions in an ever-expanding range of sectors internationally. What's more, women's tastes and preferences are transforming sectors from computers and cars to finance and fuel. Companies ignore this shift in buying power at their peril, because their smart competitors are paying close attention to women's growing influence on the market.

1. For US statistics, see http://management.fortune.cnn.com/2013/03/27/college-graduation-gender-salaries/; for international statistics, see http://www.oecd.org/edu/highlights.pdf.

So why are so many companies still struggling to adapt?

To begin with, organizations are still run mostly by men, and most people don't really understand why. Men usually point the finger at women. Women mostly point the finger at men. Companies, managers and women all feel frustrated. Some sectors still think the whole gender issue is largely irrelevant to their current male-dominated customer realities. But the truth is, gender balance benefits every company. It's time to get to the bottom of why such strong imbalances still persist and make the changes that will benefit men, women – and business as a whole.

FRONTLINE FEEDBACK: *"We keep saying that we want to more clearly mirror our consumers in terms of nationality and gender. Yet all of the senior decision makers are men, even in the product areas most closely associated with women."*

What's Your Gender Framework?

The medium is the message, Marshall McLuhan famously said. When it comes to gender issues, context is everything. Here are two very different contextual frameworks that we see in companies. They yield entirely different outcomes. Which of the following statements does your company use to frame the gender issue?

- *Framework 1:* Gender balance is a great business opportunity. It's a strong, company-wide push personally led by the CEO who is convinced that better gender balance will improve business performance.

- *Framework 2:* Gender diversity is an important diversity dimension, led by the firm's most senior woman, who is focused on improving the number of women in leadership.

Since context is such a key ingredient to successful gender balancing, it is best to have it strategically debated–and decided–by the right people. The ones with the power to actually make change happen. How important is the issue for your business, sector and stakeholders? Is it a strategic business priority, up there with some of the other key challenges the company faces? Or is it seen as a subset of diversity issues and delegated to HR or to a women's network?

A company's implementation strategy–including who is actually responsible and accountable for gender balancing–is a direct result of the initial framework. If your firm sees gender as a "women's issue" led by women and positions it as a subset of diversity issues it's unlikely to shift statistics or make changes that matter in the long term.

FRONTLINE FEEDBACK: *"In the past, there were leaders who created distrust and competitive behaviours, and functioned in a siloed approach. We're now undergoing a strategic transition, which demands a new way of working and a new leadership style. People need to understand each other's businesses and work in a way that is much more integrated and aligned. It's about a different core of values and behaviours."*

Asking the right questions of the right people is key to setting up an effective gender-balancing effort. This is more of a change management process than a diversity issue, so it helps to start at the top to ensure alignment. Then you will need to get all managers on board while simultaneously adapting the organization's policies and procedures.

Here are a few of the questions that each segment of the workforce will have to answer:

- *Senior executives.* Are the company's leaders convinced and aligned that gender is a strategic priority for the business? Do they understand the implications and leadership consequences if they decide to proactively push for balance?
- *Middle management.* Are all managers, both male and female, on board with the goal and why it has been set? Do they have the management skills and the understanding of gender differences to be able to implement an actual shift in the current balance?
- *HR and talent management.* Are HR and talent management policies aligned to support and facilitate the goals? Leadership development and identification, flexibility, career management, sponsorship, mobility and dual careers are some examples of issues and policies that can block balance efforts. Each of these needs to be reviewed and gender "neutralized" (more on this in chapter 7).
- *Sales and marketing.* Are the sales and marketing teams able to understand the benefits of gender differences and to maximize the business opportunities they offer? Men and women have different preferences and behaviours at every step of the customer journey, from website and

channel management to social media and shopping experiences. Are those variations fully understood and addressed? Are traditionally male dominated categories being examined to determine if the gender balance of their customers, end users and stakeholders are shifting? If they are, are managers prepared to make changes?

To summarize, first, gender balance becomes a business imperative: it's an opportunity for growth, rather than a diversity problem. Second, accountability for improving gender balance puts the focus on leaders and leadership, not on women. In order for real changes to happen in a company, all organizational functions and levels need to be aligned.

Identify Your Framework

Before we move on, take a minute to identify your own framework in Figure 1-1. The most common framework we encounter when meeting with a new client is the one on the left. The one we then try to build is the one on the right. Which element is your company already doing well, and where could it improve?

Figure 1-1
Evaluate your gender framework

Twentieth-century perspective	Twenty-first-century leadership
• Gender initiatives are led by women, geared for women, and branded to appeal to women. They might be called "Women's leadership seminar" or "Empowering women workshop." • Focus is more on internal talent issues than on external customer ones. • Leaders are called gender-equality "champions" or "sponsors" but are not accountable for imbalances in customer or talent profiles. • Lack of balance is a problem and a risk (in terms of lawsuits, regulation, quotas, and so on). • The end goal is equality.	• Gender is a business opportunity, not a "women's issue." • Focus is on equipping managers with skills to create gender-balanced connections to 100 percent of potential customers. • Leaders are equipped with skills to work gender bilingually with 100 percent of the talent pipeline. • Gender-balancing efforts are focused on the majority of leaders and managers, not on women in particular. • Lack of balance robs the company of important opportunities. • The end goal is competitive advantage.

2. Redefine Gender Balance

Part of the challenge in reframing gender issues is recognizing that the world – and the subject – have changed. Much of what has been done for the past twenty years on the topic is now obsolete given the dramatic shift in global gender realities. Talking about "gender diversity" in a world where women are a dominant market force isn't just out of date, it's dangerous.

The term "gender diversity" itself is a misnomer. How many genders are there? Companies are either balanced or imbalanced. The idea of gender diversity may have seemed logical in the 1980s when women were still a minority in the business world. But today, when women have become the majority of the talent and the majority of many companies' customers, is it logical to refer to them as a "diversity" dimension?

Few managers are familiar with the science, the data, or the debates surrounding gender issues. The often adversarial perspective of a "war between the sexes" portrayed by the media may be their only introduction to a subject that now often concerns more than half their employees and more than half their customers. This lack of understanding requires education and attention. Simply setting targets to bring more "women into management" does not help leaders learn how to manage across genders; rather, it usually builds a solid wall of resistance among the male majority within a company.

FRONTLINE FEEDBACK: *"We realized that it's sometimes a difficult topic to talk about. It was also clear that change does not happen overnight. It's not just about filling a few positions. To make real change, it's easier said than done. We got a better understanding of what it takes."*

Companies are failing to take advantage of the global talent and purchasing power of women, in part because of the way gender issues were positioned from the start: as a diversity dimension, with women seen as one minority among many. While nearly every large American multinational has a "diversity and inclusion" department, few have achieved anything close to real gender balance. The other challenge with "diversity" in many companies is that it is so often focused on promoting more women. Companies try to hide an urgent focus on "women" that might displease the majority of their male employees by labelling it with a more "inclusive" term. This backfires as managers are then even more frustrated by the misuse of terms, and claim–quite rightly–that "diversity is much more than gender."

FRONTLINE FEEDBACK: *"The CEO's Gender Commission is all women; he needs to invite three male leaders. Part of the misunderstanding of the issue is an antiquated view of whose responsibility it is. It's men's."*

One other important note: equal does not mean the same. Most of today's managers, both men and women, were educated to think that the very idea of gender differences was a regressive idea, steeped in stereotypes. Being progressive meant treating everyone exactly the same. Progressive managers always tell me that they "couldn't care less whether someone is male or female. Only competence counts." Yet we are discovering through all kinds of sciences – neurological, biological, psychological and physiological – that men and women are different. And today's women are confident enough to ask that those differences be recognized, understood and adapted to.

FRONTLINE FEEDBACK: *"When you walk into an office, you can smell and breathe when there is a culture that allows for good gender balance – and when there's not."*

Before you decide how to implement any change, it's useful to define what you're after and what success will look like. Clarity, transparency and prioritization are the best protection against backlash. When you're promoting gender balance, explain why you've chosen that term and what you expect the benefits to be for your company's bottom line.

Bundle Gender Balance Initiatives

Many companies are uncomfortable focusing specifically on gender. This is especially difficult in traditionally male-dominated sectors where an outright focus on gender is not always well received. Unless the gender balance issue is urgent and very obvious within your sector (for example, if 80 percent of your customers and consumers are women and 80 percent of your leaders are men), I recommend bundling gender-balance improvements with other strategic change initiatives.

FRONTLINE FEEDBACK: *"We need to begin by clarifying the facts and working through the upfront analysis. We need to understand what is the balance of men and women by region, by country, by function and level. As with any other strategic business issue, we need to segment the issue, understand the business impact and set priorities. Only then can we tackle gender balance in a clear, focused way, with a strategic program and clear actions. Otherwise it is just a lot of words, with no real substance."*

For example, many multinational companies are pushing to hire more Asian and Latin American executives. Executives recognize this as simply keeping pace with the way the world is changing–even though they don't necessarily intuitively grasp the same logic behind gender balance. Therefore, it can help to reframe gender balance as akin to the globalization push. Understanding, serving and representing gender becomes like understanding, serving and representing another country or culture. Both have to do with changing market realities.

Alternatively, gender balance can be framed as part of an effort to make technology-driven or manufacturing-driven companies more focused on building customer relationships. Or as a push toward cultivating a more progressive leadership culture that is based less on command-and-control hierarchies and more on responsive, networked and stakeholder-respecting values.

The number of companies I have seen roll out policies and communications that pair women and gender issues with disability issues is remarkable, labelling them, as I have often seen, "women and handicapped" initiatives. This positioning couldn't be more unhelpful or counterproductive. It smacks of unstrategic, diversity-led political correctness at its worst.

It's much better to repeat the message that no manager will debate: You want to reflect internally the markets you serve externally, and to do this, you need to attract the world's best talent–which most certainly includes women.

Clearly Identify Your Goal

Most companies regularly communicate statements about their diversity initiatives aimed at women. And yet very few executive teams reflect actual gender balance. Organizations must learn to be more transparent and open about their gender-balancing plans. The less clear companies are about their gender goals, the less likely they are to reach them.

Very few companies have websites that don't present statements about their initiatives aimed at women. And very few companies have executive teams that reflect actual gender balance. Organizations must learn to be more transparent and open about their gender-balancing plans. The less clear companies are about their gender goals, the less likely they are to achieve them.

Figure 2-1
Which approach does your company use?

Diversity and inclusion	**Gender balance**
• Includes all components of human differences. • Broadness of the goal makes it hard to measure success. • Little clarity about priorities across different diversity dimensions. • Creates a backlash if the focus is primarily gender, but the topic is masked as one of overall "diversity." • Organization-wide targets result in a stacking of women in support functions (PR, HR, etc.) in an attempt to get the aggregate figures to acceptable levels. • Gender and diversity both end up seen as side issues that distract managers from the real business of the organization.	• Focuses on the benefits that a balance of men and women brings to the business, to teams, and to customers. • Can be measured by asking: "Does the gender balance of our management reflect our customers, end users, and stakeholders?" • Gets the topic of gender out into the open, where managers can talk frankly about it. • Asks whether all business units and teams are balanced, with a healthy proportion of both men and women in each. • Gender balance is associated with other strategic issues, like the nationality balance of top leadership teams, deeper customer understanding, and smarter innovation.

PART 2

Focus on Your Majority

3. Build Support at the Top

The single most predictive element of the success of a gender initiative is leadership. In companies that successfully rebalance, the issue of gender balance is strongly and visibly led by the CEO. The CEO understands that the minds he needs to change are mostly among his existing (and usually male-dominated) management teams, and that those people will require strong convincing by someone who is perceived as credible.

> **FRONTLINE FEEDBACK:** *"Two years ago the CEO said [gender] was on his agenda, and that has created a real behaviour change in the company."*

Yet most companies give the leadership roles for their gender initiatives either to their most senior woman (who often heads up HR), to their women's network, or to the head of diversity. This approach simply serves to underline that it is a women's issue or a diversity dimension rather than a business priority. (The exception is in companies where the head of diversity reports directly to the CEO and is effectively positioned as a strategic change agent.)

FRONTLINE FEEDBACK: *"I think that leadership is the main stumbling block. It has to come from the top. The women's network has delivered a whole bunch of recommendations, and they were all laughed off with somewhat snide remarks. Nothing is going to change until that group visibly changes its attitude."*

Start Smart

For companies that feel like they are behind on the diversity push and who don't even have a head of diversity, congratulations. That offers an opportunity to avoid some of the mistakes from which we have learned. One of them is about how to lead the change.

Rather than setting up a separate diversity committee or women's committee with dedicated resources, I recommend that companies instead assemble small, temporary, twenty-first-century leadership task forces. This is an efficient, flexible team with the knowledge and authority to make decisions and the seniority and business networks to influence key stakeholders. Such a team would emphasize the accountability of business leaders for making change happen.

FRONTLINE FEEDBACK: *"Every Country Head should be leading on this topic, but I don't know if they really are. We need alignment. Some are real believers, others are sceptics."*

Setting up diversity committees has deflected responsibility away from the people with the clout to implement change. Over the past decade, HR teams have been launching countless initiatives, doing a lot of research, setting up women's networks, running women's conferences, applying for awards and establishing mentoring programs. Many are disillusioned – and tired. They feel like they understand the issues, that they've been struggling to get traction for years and are impatient with their bosses for the lack of gender balance evident at each new restructuring or round of promotions. They've been doing their job, so why don't the executives walk their talk?

Because CEOs don't buy it. Nor have most done enough to sell it. Here are three typical reactions, from three different companies, excerpted from the Qualitative and Quantitative QuickScan Audits we routinely do as a first step to analysing where companies stand on gender issues:

- "Top leadership says it's important, but they aren't following up with the actions to support that strategic importance."
- "We are doing this out of a sense of duty rather than any sense of conviction. So far it's been a scorecard issue."
- "This issue is *not at all* related to business. Is it an opportunity? No, that means we would discriminate the other way around. In politics, it's OK to set quotas, we need rules because it's a power issue; not in business, it's a profit motive. So if gender were good for profits, companies would be better balanced already."

In almost every session I run (in every company, in every country), the analysis of the top teams on the work that still needs to be done to promote gender balance is usually the same. The obstacles to achieving that balance typically cited by managers are a lack of skills in managing across genders and the mind-sets of the managers themselves. Managers either don't understand or aren't aware of the business case for more balance or don't understand or aren't aware of gender differences themselves. So while many companies may be tired of hearing about a topic they feel they have been working on for decades, most firms have not even started the real work.

Sell the "Why" to the Senior Team

Why does your company want to achieve better gender balance? Your leaders need to make sense of this goal. Cisco CEO John Chambers sent a letter to his staff in 2013 announcing that "the result of creating a more equal environment will not just be better performance for our organizations, but quite likely greater happiness for all."

Does his team buy this? Many progressive leaders don't think they need to explain the "why" of gender balance. To them, it is a very obvious benefit to their businesses. But most managers don't share this belief (if they did, more companies would be balanced already). And until they do – or your leaders have changed their minds – you can push all you like but are unlikely to improve your balance more in the next decade than you have in the past one.

Here is a series of reactions from a single leadership team on why gender balance is strategically smart for your business. You can see the range of opinions and general lack of alignment:

- I would rate gender balance as one of the top five factors for the company to succeed.
- Gender balance is very important in order for the company to grow.
- I believe the success of this organization will depend on greater gender balance.
- Yes, gender balance helps performance, but the benefit is not significant.
- Gender balance is a tactic that supports our strategy; it is not a strategy or an end in itself. We get no prizes for being gender balanced.
- Hmmmmmm, not sure.

Companies that successfully gender balance do so because their leaders believe it will improve quality, culture, performance and the bottom line – and they spend a lot of time and effort selling that belief to their colleagues. Do your managers get it? Do they buy it? Will they sell it to their colleagues? Take a look at figure 3-1, and see where your leaders stand.

Figure 3-1
Gender Journey: Where is your company?

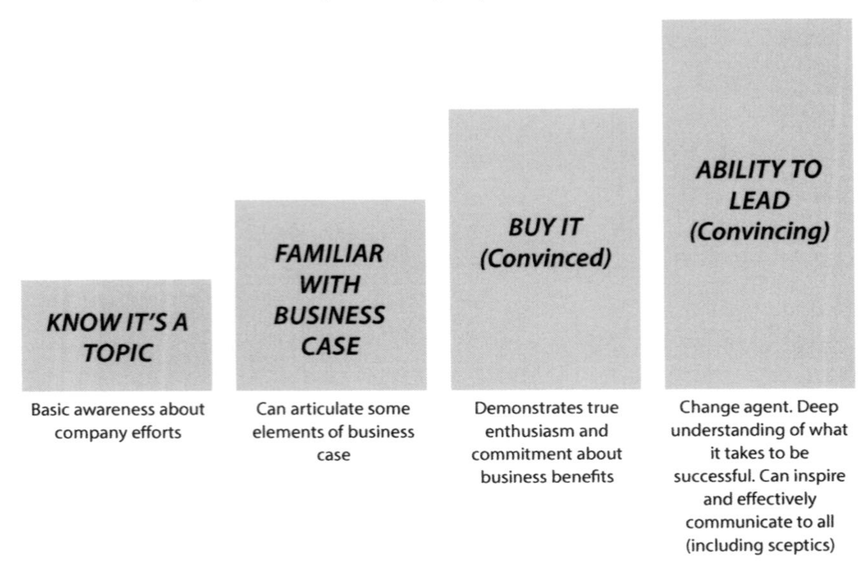

Prepare the CEO

A rarely understood challenge is getting the CEO to play his (or, more rarely, her) part in the change. While strong CEO leadership is the number one criterion for successful gender balancing, not much has been written on the nature of leadership needed.[1] Truly progressive men may not always be effective leaders on gender issues due to four blind spots that may influence their effectiveness. These blind spots can be addressed by building CEOs' awareness of their attitude and its impact.

1. A recent addition is Elisabeth Kelan's "Winning Hearts and Minds, How CEOs Talk about Gender Parity; a report sponsored by KPMG, January 2014, http://www.kpmg.com/ulden/issuesandinsights/articlespublications/pages/winning-hearts-and-minds.aspx.

It's a no-brainer

Some intuitively progressive CEOs consider the case for gender balance so obvious that it doesn't require elaboration or argument. These leaders don't think they need to convince anyone of the benefits of balance. They don't think anyone needs to hear any kind of business case anymore – that is yesterday's battle. They assume their teams are all aligned behind them, and all they need to do is communicate a target. Such CEOs usually launch enthusiastically into the fray, over-communicating their goal and underestimating the incomprehension that usually meets their efforts. They end up frustrated a couple of years later at the lack of progress. These leaders often waste precious time and goodwill on ineffective approaches that respond to a partial understanding of the underlying issues and don't take into account the potential reaction from their male majorities. Essentially, they charge out of the closet – and into a buzz of backlash.

As a result, these leaders often take overly aggressive approaches with unrealistic timelines. They either revisit the topic with more appropriate resourcing after a few years of unsatisfactory progress, or a successor quietly shelves their efforts.

It's not worth fighting for (or being identified with)

Other CEOs are quiet supporters but don't want to make it a big deal. It's kind of like religion: something to be practiced quietly at home but not discussed in public.

This point of view is probably the one most commonly held by the progressive men I've met. Yet this majority status makes these men crucial to changing the cultures of the companies and countries where they work. Moreover, these individuals are currently developing, promoting and financing tomorrow's talent. This requires the skills and engagement to be proactively leading on gender issues. Yet in many of the sessions I run, it is the nay-sayers that are loud, assertive and argumentative. The progressive men hold back, occasionally suggesting a caveat to a reactionary's voluble bluster. It takes a lot of courage for men to stand up to other men on the topic of gender balancing.

Too many progressive men are taken aback by some of the heated reactions they encounter and often decide that gender is not enough of a priority to fight for. So they let louder voices dominate – and then drown – the debate.

It will happen naturally

Some leaders argue that it is a simple case of meritocracy: recognizing and promoting the best people. They assume that, since the pipeline of colleges, graduate programs and entry- to mid-level jobs are full of high-performing women, merit will win out and eventually women will start to make it in real numbers to the senior levels. Just as they have seen in their own teams. They think the issue is on its way to being solved naturally, without intervention.

In doing so, they underestimate their own skills and gender bilingualism. They don't see that their own ability to recognize talent equally well among both men and women is an unusual skill that not all managers possess. They are usually reluctant to spend much time and effort equipping others with the skills and awareness that they themselves take for granted. This blind spot has much the same effect as the others: ineffective leadership on the issue.

I'm a champion, but not the right person to spearhead the effort

Many progressive men still view any mention of the word "gender" as being about women, and they feel they should defer to female leadership on the topic. They ask their most senior women to take the visible leadership role, and they become "champions" or "sponsors" of the effort. They typically give the introductory remarks at their women's networks' events and meet with senior women to listen to their feedback, but they will rarely engage with their peers or other men on the topic at all. This reinforces the perspective that gender balance is an issue that is entirely in the hands of women, and that leaders have no accountability or responsibility on the topic, aside from encouraging the gals on.

If you're reading this and recognize any of your own impulses here, there are specific actions you can take to have more influence on this issue:

- *Build self-awareness.* Learn how to lead on gender, or become more aware of how you're already doing it. Ask for feedback from your team about how your management style may differ from others they have experienced.
- *Know the data.* Take the time to do the research on the gender balance within your sector and company. What is the male/female ratio of your customers? And your workforce?
- *Sell the idea.* Recognize that your colleagues may not buy into the idea of balance. Be prepared to sell it.
- *Role model the "how."* Be aware that even if your colleagues like the idea of gender balance, they may

not know how to get there. Teach them what you know.

- *Let men lead the charge on gender balancing – not "champion" it from the sidelines.* If you've decided to make this a serious initiative at your firm, bravo! Just don't appoint a woman to head the project. Male majorities are likely to buy the business case for gender balance better from a man, at least in the first phase.
- *Hold leaders accountable.* Set benchmarks and measure progress in attaining balance, and set up consequences for inaction.

4. Get Leaders to Lead

To shift the gender balance, leaders need to ask the right people the right questions. Rather than ask women why they are not being promoted, it helps to ask the people actually doing the promoting. Rather than getting women to devise strategies to improve gender balance, get leaders involved in the analysis and implementation of action plans. Then make them accountable for change. Rather than expecting women to adopt the current, top-down business model, why not question the relevance of the model in today's business landscape and get men and women to redesign it together for a gender balanced twenty-first century?

For a shift of this kind to take place, it is imperative to start at the top, usually by spending a day with the executive team.

Most executive teams are not convinced of the business case for gender balance, even though the CEO might be. They are largely unaware of the latest statistics on women's economic power as employees and customers. These numbers may have been presented before but are not always conveyed in a convincing, business-driven way by the right kind of spokesperson, or they have been part of more-general briefings on diversity that drown the message.

FRONTLINE FEEDBACK: *"Deep down in my heart I wonder if this extreme focus on gender is much ado about nothing. The gender profile has been the same for decades and is probably very similar at other companies, yet the business goes on."*

The (usually majority male) executive team members rarely have been asked to debate or analyse the issue of gender balance, and unless there is some form of experiential buy-in at this level, little progress is likely.

Spend a day with these executive teams in sessions that can then be rolled out to their direct reports and key executive and managerial populations. This is more about creating buy-in and alignment than it is about training. Only companies willing to invest in building gender bilingualism among their leaders will be in a position to realistically implement the changes around gender as a business issue that are required to make real, sustainable progress.

How can you ensure an honest debate? It is essential that the CEO open with a heartfelt, authentic invitation to employees to avoid political correctness and say what they really think about this topic. It should be positioned as a go, no-go debate, where the team will decide whether or not to focus on the issue going forward. The CEO's candor may be a great relief to those who have been frustrated by the problem over many years but not known what to do about it. Of course, if the team has pre-existing issues of trust or if the CEO lacks credibility, this may not be the easiest topic to work through. Occasionally, especially with relatively new CEOs, it can become a theme that brings out entirely new kinds of conversations and connections and reveals team members to each other in ways that can be very helpful in team building.

It helps to prepare and brief the CEO before such a meeting. His (and even more her) role is all-important in creating an atmosphere of trust and communication. In general, you will want the CEO to take a back seat during much of the debate, to be able to listen and map out where his or her colleagues are in terms of their mind-sets, understanding and attitudes. That should be one of the major goals for these sessions: to learn how big the change management journey will be, who is likely to have the most trouble with it, and how much appetite or resistance there will be to the change. This is essential for the CEO to measure before launching the roadmap for each company's – and each executive team's – gender journey.

If the executive team is not prepared to take the time or spend the money for this debate, that is a pretty good indicator that the company is unlikely to be ready to invest in making the other adaptations that a balanced approach requires. Non-strategic gender initiatives can do more harm than good by raising – and then failing to meet – expectations. In this case, take some time out. Let competitors and customers heighten the pressure, and/or identify and then build coalitions with powerful internal change agents; then revisit the topic later.

A Process for Leading Change

If the executive team is prepared to devote real resources to gender balance, the CEO should invite group members to air their views honestly. Political correctness is the death of the gender dialogue. The team should acquire relevant data, review their internal realities, and debate the gender issue and its strategic relevance for their organizations. It should get expert input into gender differences, discuss how the company is currently integrating them, and brainstorm ways to improve their business through a more strategic approach to those differences. The team can then craft an action plan, complete with defined objectives, timetables and accountability–and commit to it.

> **FRONTLINE FEEDBACK:** *"I have no idea what my colleagues think. I have never talked about gender in my life."*

When the executive team is ready to roll out their plan throughout the company, it is essential to keep peer groups together so that employees feel comfortable airing their real opinions and work together to make change in their own teams. This can result in many male-dominated leadership team sessions. Companies often want to bring a few women into these debates to improve the balance or representation of views, but if women are not already part of the team, that is not a useful tactic at this stage. The objective is to get leaders to understand the gender issue and to define how significant a priority it is for their business. These sessions have three major objectives, aimed at launching a momentum for change.

1. Find Out Who Cares

Companies that are seriously ready to push gender balance usually have a CEO who is personally convinced of the need to move forward and create impact, starting at the top. The CEO is usually also convinced that his executive team is aligned behind him. But because the gender issue is often either mired in political correctness or seen as a minor HR issue, the real pros and cons of rebalancing gender have rarely been debated at this level. Dissent has never been aired, and alignment among the leadership team is often simply assumed–but may not exist.

FRONTLINE FEEDBACK: *"Leadership says gender is a top priority, because there is a lot of political correctness surrounding the subject. But they don't really believe it's that important. The action that I've witnessed to date is unconvincing. If it were really important then it would be defined as one of our top 5 or 10 priorities, and we would be executing differently."*

Alignment is not obvious. In fact, I've never seen it. The misguided belief that everyone agrees on gender balance is a significant barrier to implementing the required changes.

To find out if your team is aligned, conduct a quick, confidential vote. Ask each executive-team member to write down, anonymously, the priority level he or she would give to gender as a business issue for their company over the next five years, on a scale of one to ten. A range of numbers is likely to emerge, immediately allowing the CEO to discover why the company has made so little progress on the issue: More than likely, it's because the firm's leaders don't agree that it should.

2. Look at the Data

Review the statistics. Do the external ones first: the reality of a shifting talent pool, customer profiles and demographic or regulatory pressures. Then do internal ones: Compare the significant, sometimes revolutionary, external evolutions with a company's internal statistics and progress over time.

The data will tell its own story. The tale won't be that of the oft-cited glass ceiling, with its assumption that women make it up through the ranks until a sudden blockage at a senior level. The reality in today's corporate world is that the percentage of women drops off at almost every level.

The glass ceiling metaphor has blinded many to a more pervasive problem – what I call "gender asbestos": Companies have not yet adapted their cultures, career paths, processes and promotions to include women. There is an invisible layer of unconscious barriers, mind-sets and corporate processes that unwittingly affect women more than men. Like asbestos, they need to be consciously identified and then rooted out. The result is that companies are still not good at identifying, retaining and promoting female talent, despite decades of attempted progress. Most of the members of the executive team are unlikely to have looked at this data in detail or been asked how it impacts the business.

FRONTLINE FEEDBACK: *"We've set targets without tackling the processes that would allow us to have the results we want. We've been lazy; making real change happen takes work:"*

The external customer story is even more compelling. Who are your customers – and potential customers – becoming? One CEO in a company in the agricultural sector was convinced that his industry was entirely male dominated. The all-male team was united in believing that female farmers were few and far between and not worth much attention as a result. Opinions changed, however, when company research revealed that a third of farmers in India and China were women, and that women were the fastest-growing segment. The same is true for a tire company that swore that its customers (and the entire category) were made up of men

– until the firm's UK operation discovered that 55 percent of their tires were actually being bought by women. Smartphones used to be considered a male segment, until Apple came along and made millions by innovating a totally gender bilingual product.

Strangely, few companies look at the gender issue holistically, as both a customer opportunity and an internal talent imperative. Because the topic is usually introduced at lower levels of the organization, it usually gets categorized either as a market issue or as a talent issue. Yet working on them together makes a lot more sense. They are not really separate issues. Having the sales and marketing team make a lot of women-friendly products and advertisements can actually backfire when women consumers learn that the company seems more challenged at promoting them than selling to them.

FRONTLINE FEEDBACK: *"We are doing this out of a sense of duty rather than any sense of conviction. So far it's been a scorecard issue."*

So invite the top team to take a big picture approach. A simple "SWOT" exercise, in which the team is asked to analyse the strengths, weaknesses, opportunities and threats of the company in rebalancing gender, should help. Most will be familiar with the process but will never have applied it to gender. This is where experiential learning comes into play.

Figure 4-1
A simple SWOT exercise can clarify leaders' views on gender

SWOT (strengths, weaknesses, opportunities, and threats) If we aim to improve our current gender balance, what is likely to happen?	
STRENGTHS What are our company's current strengths that will facilitate this effort?	**WEAKNESSES** What are our company's current weaknesses that may challenge this effort?
OPPORTUNITIES What business benefits do we believe better balance will capture?	**THREATS** What are some of the risks of pushing forward on this topic?

The experiential learning will come not only from the debate among peers about the data's significance and whether they should care about it, but also when the mostly male members of the team hear their colleagues' positions on the topic. Using this short SWOT exercise, it will become intensely clear and unavoidably visible what each individual thinks of gender, how comfortable they are or aren't discussing–let alone leading on–the issue, and which of three management segments they fall into. These segments include:

- *Progressive:* gets the business case and is convinced that balancing is a business imperative
- *Patient:* ready to keep pace with external realities but unlikely to believe in a proactive approach
- *Plodding:* sceptical of any business link and often ready to block, undermine, or simply ignore any efforts toward change.

Nothing is more powerful for the progressives in the room than to hear a group of "plodding" colleagues use arguments they thought had disappeared a generation ago. It's usually a strong wake up call for the CEO to become aware of this and goes a long way to explaining any lack of progress and the reality of the challenge that lies ahead.

3. Make a Plan

The day should conclude with action planning. After an executive team has been through this kind of workshop, it will probably agree that new initiatives need to be rolled out to all executives and managers throughout the company.

The team will have identified the key drivers and frameworks for the topic. What is the goal, by when and why? Will it be bundled together with other global change initiatives? Will it have a strong customer dimension? Is talent the driving force for change? What is the business case in this company? How will they follow up with next steps? Another important question is who will lead the charge. As I've stated, the executive team should choose a male leader to spearhead the efforts–someone who is respected throughout the company.

Rebalancing gender in leadership does not require a decades-long investment in training women to adopt behaviours that are more acceptable to the dominant norm. A better approach is to invite the dominant norm to better understand, articulate and sell why its interests lie in maximizing the opportunities of all of the potential market. Now real progress can begin.

Which approaches has your firm already tried?

Figure 4-2
Launch your gender initiative strategically to see better results

Traditional launch	Strategic launch
• Position gender as a part of wider diversity initiatives. • Give gender initiatives titles such as "Women in Leadership," clearly positioning them as a women's issue, not a business issue. • Think of women as a minority. • Appoint a woman to run the gender issue. • Create a women's network as the key initiative. • Ask women for proposals to improve gender balance. • Promote women, as long as they behave as much like men as possible. • Disconnect initiative from markets, customers, and stakeholders.	• Start by getting the executive team and CEO to debate the issue. • Position it as a business issue, not as a women's issue. • Get top management to design and approve the goal, the urgency, and the action plan. • Appoint a high-profile senior man to run the gender initiative. • Position gender outside of diversity and HR, recognizing sales and marketing as key players. • Think of women as a majority. • Train men (and women) how to manage "bilingually" across genders. • Train men (and women) to sell bilingually across genders.

5. Equip Leaders to Be Convinced and Convincing

During these executive team meetings, leaders generally become far more convinced about the business benefits of more gender balance than they were previously. For some, it is a veritable eye-opener. Leaving the session, however, they need to be not only convinced but also convincing. A key next step is for leaders to sell their decisions and action plans to their teams and colleagues.

Executives can benefit from doing some planning and research to make their case convincing. Here is a short, to-the-point toolkit of ready-to-use supports.

> Make Your Message on Gender Effective
>
> **Key messages to convey:**
>
> - Why should others care? What's the benefit of balance?
> - What gender differences affect our business?
> - How are we planning to adapt?
>
> **Data to support the "why" argument:**
>
> - Customer data and profiling
>   - Potential customer data
>   - Competitor customer comparisons
>   - Customer focus group feedback on current company image, products and services, broken down by gender
> - Talent data and profiling
>   - Attraction, retention and promotion statistics, broken down by gender

Conciseness and relevance here is key. The clearer leaders are about their message and the data behind it, the more likely they will succeed in aligning their teams behind them. Clarity around the basic message and data hugely enables strong and impactful global roll-outs.

Get Majority Buy-In

The real obstacle in many companies is not women. It is the existing leadership mind-set, culture and styles–usually dominated by men. This means most of your attention will need to be focused on your male majority, not your female minority. You will need to get all your people to understand why change is important and why it hasn't happened in the past.

FRONTLINE FEEDBACK: *"In order to have true success, everyone needs to believe. The CEO and his direct reports get it. However, below this level the messaging needs improvement, especially around the 'why.' The next level below needs to demonstrate the same commitment as the top team. The basic awareness is missing!"*

I have seen companies spend time and money focusing gender awareness on middle management, while their top teams' styles and behaviours undermine the message and prove a lack of commitment. Senior leaders are particularly essential for evolving the attitudes of male middle managers, who will be watching to see how any changes might be politically relevant to their own careers. If the leaders who will be promoting and rewarding them are not serious about the shift, employees won't be either.

Take the time to explain *why* the change is necessary. Repeat the format and debate that was carried out with the leadership teams. It is important that both the rational arguments and the more emotional reactions have time to air. Middle managers and other employees may not have the big picture view available to those at the top. In some companies and countries, the gender issues become easier as you cascade to a broader (and younger) group of managers, but in most organizations it becomes harder. Don't underestimate the need to cascade awareness and skill building to all levels.

FRONTLINE FEEDBACK: *"Male managers are neutral, disengaged; some are slightly apprehensive about what it means for them. We are observers, rather than participants. It feels a bit like a women's agenda (or sometimes a senior management agenda). It's not easy to get engaged."*

Information that covers questions and issues relevant to all workers will need to be bundled into onboarding programs as well as management and leadership development programs. The more these can be combined strategically with leadership subjects, strategic marketing, or talent management, the better. Just like the initial framework, where these sessions appear and in what context will be as important as their content. So, for example, don't put gender issues into a day on diversity management. Instead include it in a week on customer centricity or on global leadership development. Vigilance is likely to be required to keep the gender issue business focused.

The current framework runs deep in many organizations, and some careful "rebranding" may be required in companies that have invested a lot in gender initiatives that have been entirely focused – and branded – as women's programs. While this may make sense for external, consumer-focused strategies, it's generally not constructive on an internal, talent-focused level.

Companies overestimate the readiness and competence of managers to deliver on gender targets. Quotas on boards are relatively easy. It is not hard to add a non-executive woman or two to a board. Gender balancing an entire organization, from the bottom all the way through to the top, however, takes management skills that are probably not yet widely developed.

We have been here before. Globalization required managers to become fluent in the languages and cultures of other countries. It took years of patient management development, usually requiring that a lot of managers live in many different countries for many years of their lives. Gender bilingualism will also take some time.

FRONTLINE FEEDBACK: *"There is a feeling at the top that gender balance is important for the company and that we definitely need to do something. But we don't actually know what to do, or how to make change happen."*

How long will it take managers to become effectively gender bilingual? Fluent enough in the differences and cultures of men and women to manage today's balanced talent pools and to sell to increasingly gender balanced markets? The answer is that it will take longer than most CEOs or HR teams are allowing for.

Companies will need to invest a bit of time and money building skills among their leaders and managers. It is hard to manage across genders when people don't really understand what the differences are and how they affect the workplace. The challenge here is not to treat everyone equally and the same (as most managers think they do), but to treat everyone equally and different, with a deep understanding of what those differences are.

FRONTLINE FEEDBACK: *"People have bought into the idea of better gender balance conceptually. But when the rubber hits the road, we just aren't able to do it."*

You don't manage employees or customers in China the same way you would manage an employee or customer in the United States or in Brazil. You learn their language and culture. You've probably spent a lot of time and money getting your company to learn about the Chinese and their customs and business practices. You'll need to build the same competencies for your managers, both male and female, to understand the differences and opportunities of gender. This requires training in gender differences, preferably with a focus on both the internal, employee dimensions and the external, customer/stakeholder dimensions.

Avoid Pointing Fingers

"Without realizing it, we operate every day with gender stereotypes and biases," Cisco CEO John Chambers has said. While this may be true, it's not the most motivating way to launch a change.

Accusing men of bias is a great way, in my experience, of shutting them down. So many popular programs are now labelled with accusatory language. Training seminars on "stereotypes," "sexual harassment," and "unconscious bias" do nothing to help the cause of promoting gender balance.

Frank Dobbin, a sociology professor at Harvard, has done a lot of research on corporate diversity programs. He has found that many "don't have any effect at all or backfire" at a cost of time and money. Dobbin says that these programs tend to alternate between two typical approaches: One is to teach managers about their own bias, an idea most people tend to resist and one that implies that managers are to blame for a lack of diversity. The other is to control managers by implementing strict rules regarding hiring and promotion. Dobbin argues that managers prefer to solve problems on their own rather than having to conform to specific guidelines. "It doesn't work to blame managers and tell them they're biased or try to control them through bureaucratic rules. That doesn't make them happy, and in the end it's not effective."

Surely there is a better way of building enthusiasm for balance than accusing people of bad behaviour before they even get into the room. It's not that these problems are not present, and need to be identified and eliminated. But they can be framed more attractively to invite enthusiasm and celebrate management competence. I would suggest framing the entire topic as a dimension of twenty-first-century leadership. Gender bilingualism, both in terms of understanding consumers better and of better talent management, can be positioned and presented as a skill that will enhance managers' own success.

FRONTLINE FEEDBACK: *"People understand gender intellectually, but are not emotionally connected to it."*

It is easy to reframe gender balance as one of the century's most obvious business opportunities. You need to get everyone aligned and focused on what everyone wins from gender balance. Framing this as a problem caused by biases is setting these efforts up to fail. Most male managers (at least in reasonably well-run companies) believe they already practice equal treatment. So asking them, as many companies do, to come up with changes will not be understood until they have gone through some phase of building understanding. What most surprises people is how fun and stimulating the gender topic can be. Every man and woman on the planet today is facing gender issues at home and at work. Helping them to understand and navigate one of human history's big revolutions doesn't have to be an accusatory man- or woman-bashing exercise. The real question is, how do we better understand each other?

FRONTLINE FEEDBACK: *"But what has been critical is the way that a better understanding of differences has allowed our team to listen better and be more open to different approaches and perspectives. People are more patient and willing to spend time to listen to different views, which is a real change. This has brought a lot to the team."*

The more strategically you can frame the issue – as a lever to achieving existing growth, customer centricity and globalization goals rather than as a politically correct addition to already over-burdened agendas – the more enthusiasm you'll generate. Gender balanced companies have better performance, better talent and better customer and stakeholder relationships. But you'll need to say it, show it, prove it and then deliver it to actually get everyone to believe it.

Run it as a women-focused diversity initiative, and you'll be at the same place a decade from now. Run it as a key driver in keeping your company in tune with twenty-first-century talent and customers, and you may make history.

Stop Fixing Women, and Shift the Question

The first reaction of companies that want to (further) improve their balance is to benchmark best practices. They discover that many companies run a myriad of much-communicated initiatives aimed at women. They don't usually try to analyse the effectiveness of these programs; they simply compete on the PR potential of running women's initiatives and how that may create an impression of balance. Yet decades of these programs have not significantly shifted the statistics.

This leads to more "women's" programs–networks, coaching and assertiveness training. This is the challenge raised by Sheryl Sandberg's recent book, *Lean In*, which created such a debate in the United States. Reading it, male leaders might reasonably conclude that women still need fixing and empowering. Yet the world has never seen a more ambitious and skilled wave of women graduate from universities. To succeed, these women just need meritocracies and companies and managers skilled in leading across genders.

To recap, here are the ground rules to follow:

- *Sell before you measure.* Convince people of the benefits before you give them targets they won't buy into.
- *Focus on the majority (men) not the minority (women).* Get all your managers to understand why they should care.
- *Put skills before scorecards.* Equip your employees with gender bilingual skills to actually execute, then give them targets.
- *Walk before you talk.* Make some progress before you start communicating externally or on your website about how balanced you are. Nothing disgruntles both men and women more than overcommunicating externally and untruthfully about gender.

The rest is (relatively) simple.

Which approach describes how your organization has approached gender balance initiatives in the past?

Figure 5-1
What's your company's gender perspective?

Traditional perspective	**Today's perspective**
"What's wrong with women? Let's help them."	What's wrong with our company if we can't attract, retain, and develop the majority of the educated talent in the world today?"
Focus on women and what they lack.	Focus on helping companies and managers adapt to the reality of women in the twenty-first century: their talents and influence on markets (60 percent of university graduates are female and 80 percent of consumer goods purchasing decisions are in the hands of women).

PART 3

Get the Systems to Match

6. The Gender Bilingual Organization

Most executive teams I work with would prefer to skip over most of what we have just covered and get directly to the "doing" of an action plan. But it doesn't make sense to jump into initiatives before the company's leadership has worked to reach agreement and alignment on goals, drivers, focus and urgency.

Half the work is to get companies to pause before they push. Gender-balancing talent and market strategies takes a few consecutive years of proactive management focus and drive. The result can be transformative on a global level. If done ineffectively, though, it can be divisive and distracting, alienate customers, or cause an unintended brain drain of one gender or the other.

Management understanding and buy-in is the essential ingredient to change. A whole range of initiatives won't have the impact they deserve if managers don't push for balance. Part of that evolution takes leadership: role models, communicating the business case, walking the talk and celebrating success. The other part requires systemic change: products and services must be researched, designed, sold and serviced with both men and women in mind. Talent management processes that use the full range of tools – development, reward, key performance indicators and feedback – are required to make the shift toward desired balance and behaviours.

This chapter gives an overview of some of the systems and policies that need to reflect the leadership commitment that may emerge – first on the talent side, then on the market side. It is essential that companies keep both the talent and the market dimensions together in working on gender. They are flip sides of the same coin. Figuring out the benefits of balance for their businesses, leaders almost always identify potential both internally and externally.

Yet most companies tend to focus their efforts on one side or the other. So does a lot of the research. There are a raft of excellent books about marketing to women, including *Why She Buys*, by Bridget Brennan; *What Women Want*, by Paco Underhill; *The Power of the Purse*, by Fara Warner; and *Inside Her Pretty Little Head*, by Jane Cunningham and Philippa Roberts. There is also a group of helpful books about women in leadership, including *Through the Labyrinth*, by Alice H. Eagly and Linda L. Carli; *Women Don't Ask*, by Linda Babcock and Sara Laschever; *Talking From 9 to 5*, by Deborah Tannen; or the recent *Lean In*, by Sheryl Sandberg. These two topics tend to be treated as though they were entirely different subjects without any overlap, as though the buyer has no relationship with who is doing the developing, designing and selling.

This is partly the result of the buyer for this research: All the leadership and talent issues are channelled into the human resources teams, while all the marketing is presented to the sales and marketing side of the business. That's another reason why it is helpful at the outset for leaders to identify the breadth of the gender opportunity for their business.

The principles remain the same for both HR and sales and marketing:

- *Understand differences.* Companies and managers need to be more informed on the differences between men and women – as talent, customers, end users and stakeholders.
- *Extrapolation kills innovation.* Simply extrapolating systems that worked for one gender to the other eliminates the innovation that comes from using gender differences to create something new: products, services, leadership styles, or company cultures.
- *Fitting in equals dropping out.* Forcing one gender to fit into pre-existing norms created by the other is not a recipe for success. It guarantees a loss of customers and talent – or at least a lot of missed opportunities for growth.
- *Balance requires both genders.* Gender issues have been either ignored or seen as male or female focused for long enough. Companies, cultures and systems must become fully gender bilingual to reach all of the market and all of the talent.

There is a mountain of research on gender differences in a broad range of sciences, from neurology and physiology to psychology to behavioural economics. The goal isn't to make an exhaustive study of every gender difference. Only the ones relevant to the business. And to reverse decades of encouraging managers to ignore gender. Because gender differences used to be steeped in stereotypes, many people are rightly concerned that focusing on differences will perpetuate them. There are endless debates about "nurture versus nature." Companies must acknowledge that differences do exist (no matter where they come from); that women are now, in many countries, empowered enough to celebrate them; and that they no longer want to be treated exactly the same as men or be promoted only if they adapt to the dominant paradigm.

You don't manage or sell to women the same way you do to men. It's only by becoming fluent in the language and culture of both genders (and the differences between them) that you will connect with anyone. Managers need to become gender bilingual to work across genders, just as they need to become multicultural in order to work across national borders and cultures.

Many of the policies and processes in companies were designed in the twentieth century by men, for men. They need twenty-first-century updating for a more balanced talent and customer base. While cultural adaptation depends a lot on leadership, unintended systemic obstacles can undermine the most progressive pushing. Policies and practices are often invisible, so taken for granted that they aren't part of most gender initiatives, yet they subtly determine behaviours and block progress.

Following is a chart that details the differences between men and women in business, as suggested by Jane Cunningham and Philippa Roberts in their excellent and highly recommended book, *The Daring Book for Boys in Business* (a tongue-in-cheek reference to one of the United Kingdom's most beloved books for boys). This is an essential read on how to adapt marketing approaches in male categories to make them more bilingual. Here I summarize some of their work and elaborate by showing how the differences they cite also affect the internal, talent management side of business.

TALENT	MALE	FEMALE	MARKET
Recruitment	Belief in machine	Belief in people	R&D, development
	Self-focused	Other focused	
Retention	Improve formula	Read audience	Customer relationships
	Expert	Girlfriend	
Promotion	Impressing	Mirroring	Communications

Source: Jane Cunningham and Philippa Roberts, The Daring Book for Boys in Business: Solving the Problem of Marketing and Branding to Women (London: LID Publishing, 2012).

- *Belief in machine versus belief in people.* Masculine messages are often aimed at describing the technology, the machine, the process or the product, sometimes in astonishing levels of detail. Messages aimed at the feminine are going to be focusing more on people, stories and relationships.
- *Self-focused versus other focused.* The masculine angle will often focus on messages that describe how a product or service will help make you "better, stronger, faster, or smarter." A more feminine positioning will suggest how the product or service will be better for those you care for, for other people, or for the planet.
- *Improve formula versus read the audience.* Masculine messages are always ready to underline even incremental improvements to the product or service. One example is how Gillette keeps adding blades to its razor for a closer shave. The feminine approach would be to demonstrate an ever-deeper understanding of the audience and its often unspoken needs, thereby unlocking innovation.

An example is the Dove ads that acknowledge women's complicated self-judgments about body image.

- *Expert versus girlfriend.* The masculine will be comfortable with companies positioning themselves as experts and will check their credibility. The feminine will prefer a position as trusted girlfriend, full of advice and similarities of understanding and perspective.
- *Impressing versus mirroring.* The masculine may be more comfortable with companies that seek to impress with their combined machines, formulas and expertise, while the feminine is going to prefer a salesperson that mirrors her own reality and understands her needs because she shares them.

7. Gender Bilingual Talent Management

The focus of a lot of gender balancing efforts a decade ago was around the paucity of balance in pipelines. So companies started recruiting far more women, expecting the balance to naturally flow through the entire system. Today, companies have realized that this has not happened and that they have to carefully analyse gender balance at every management level, across different functions and throughout the entire career cycle of their managers.

FRONTLINE FEEDBACK: *"There is nothing in the organization that prepares male managers to understand women and see their potential."*

It is important to analyse where the gaps start, where they widen and what they mean, from recruitment and retention to promotion and leadership. Many companies have not yet deepened their analysis to this level of granularity.

Recruitment

Most companies adopt aggregate targets that over-focus on women, excluding men from the subject. For example, Germany's DAX 30 companies have set a target of 30 percent women in management. The danger with such targets is that they push companies to recruit a lot of younger women all of a sudden, which leaves them with a new problem when they have a large number of middle managers all hitting their child-bearing years at the same time. They also tend to end up with strange gender ghettos in certain functions, with a dominance of women in support departments and a dominance of men in operational roles. This creates a new and often more difficult problem to solve over time.

It is good to take a long-term view of the pacing and goal setting of gender initiatives, one that focuses on balance and the acceptable ratios of men to women at every age, stage and area of the business – rather than one that simply focuses on global aggregate averages of women in management. Here are some ways to get more granular and understand your own company's recruiting impacts in detail.

Let Your Corporate Website Emphasize People as well as Products

A quick look at a company's corporate website–now the major communications channel for any potential recruit–is often enough to determine whether products and machines dominate the culture or whether the organization is more people oriented. This is usually illustrated by a lot of pictures of machines, innovations, or products, often with a surprising absence of any pictures of people at all. The belief in the machine is patent in many scientific or engineering-based companies, which wonder why they have trouble attracting more women.

FRONTLINE FEEDBACK: *"Maybe we are having trouble attracting the right female candidates because of the signals we are giving that this is not a place for women to succeed, since there are only men in top management."*

One company we worked with was so proud of its sophisticated helicopters that there was not a single human face on its entire site. Companies may try to correct for this by adding some stock photos of people who are so obviously more diverse (one black individual, one Asian person, a few women) than the reality in their company that it simply communicates the company's inauthenticity and political correctness. If they have real photos of people, it usually communicates a surprising lack of diversity–and the organization tends to be dominated by men.

Gender bilingual websites portray an authentic balance of impressive products and people who workers would want to mirror.

Use the Right Language

The language of recruitment ads and the "careers" pages of websites is another good place to check for "self-centred" or "expert" male preferences. A lot of recruitment advertising appeals to what an individual stands to gain by joining the company. Related language might be, "Join us and you will become bigger, stronger, faster and smarter." A more feminine preference would be to invite potential recruits to join in an endeavour that will serve a larger purpose. Language in this case might be, "Join us and together we will make the world better, greener and safer . . ."

In both of these cases, a gender bilingual approach would be to encompass male and female styles. Google's career tagline, "Do cool things that matter," shows this well. Many companies have not yet learned the differences and subtleties of the messages, language and styles that may be attractive to men and women. They tend to simply extrapolate what they have used historically for their dominant majority. It takes quite a lot of thought and adaptation to be attractive to today's younger, female-dominated educated talent. Companies will first want to raise awareness of the different motivators of both men and women and then integrate them into every part of the recruitment chain – from communication channels to on-campus recruiting events to vocabulary and role models.

Focus on Retention

Retaining talented women once you've hired them is more complicated than just creating a "women's network" in your firm. Here are several other approaches that are more effective.

Provide Role Models

Companies often think that displaying the presence of senior women will be enough to attract other women. But it is not that simple. Both men and women can be powerful aspirational role models if they carry gender bilingual values and can connect by both impressing and mirroring. Men who can talk about both their personal and their professional lives can effectively mirror many women's preferences to integrate these dimensions more flexibly than most corporate men have historically been allowed to. I asked several managers in companies I've worked with to describe what a leader is like in their organization. Their responses may not surprise you–but will probably depress you.

- "In our company, a leader is driven, competitive, workaholic, a road warrior, driven by results, un-empathetic."
- "We have a very networked culture. You're in or out. People who succeed are the ones who shout the loudest in meetings and who spend the most time showcasing themselves. The silent soldiers have a tougher time."
- "Someone who can deliver the numbers. That's the summary."

Too many of the senior women that companies offer as role models are often in fact anti-role models, as they are perceived as having adapted too much to the dominant male corporate culture and have become overly masculine in their leadership style. Senior male leaders are often unable to tell the difference between women who are or are not role models to the next generation of women. Naturally impressed by women who have adapted to male styles, they don't understand that it is precisely this adaptation that renders them less attractive to a younger generation that no longer wants to adapt. This is a huge part of the retention problem in many companies. Young female talent is hungry for mirrors: older women who echo their concerns and choices and can illustrate that they have found a way to remain authentically themselves and still be successful in the organization. Sadly, this is a major issue in many companies.

Today's workforce needs gender bilingual role models, where both male and female managers become skilled in "impressing" intellectually and "mirroring" emotionally.

FRONTLINE FEEDBACK: *"For me personally, there are no female role models. A few successful women, but no role models. To succeed, a woman has to be more like a man than a woman. We do not respect more feminine behaviour or leadership styles."*

Offer Flexibility

Systems, rather than people, have long dominated where and how people work. What companies produce and the systems that have traditionally been necessary to deliver it often determine today's working hours and requirements. So manufacturing-based businesses tend to be tied to very rigid hours (and rigid management mind-sets) dictated by factory production cycles. The high-tech sector is an exception, as a flexible work environment is in sync with the products they provide: the ability to work anytime, anywhere. Service companies whose major assets are people have been far readier to integrate the "people" dimension into work than capital-intensive businesses seeking to optimize expensive manufacturing systems.

FRONTLINE FEEDBACK: *"At senior levels, the demands and expectations (travel, work ethic, hours) become very intense. Although the CEO has sent a strong message that he is more interested in output than how many air miles you've racked up, there is still a very male badge of honour regarding intense travel ('I've been on three continents in three weeks'). It is really important to stress this is not just a gender issue. I know several younger high potential guys who are saying `thanks but no thanks' to this psychological contract."*

Flexibility, both in terms of working style and in terms of career management throughout people's lives, is often divided by this belief in either systems or people. Gender balancing inevitably requires adapting rigid work styles that were developed to maximize machine efficiency to the flexible realities of people's complex and multidimensional lives today. Recently I was speaking to a factory manager in Brazil who told me he simply could not make his factory's schedule more flexible or offer any part-time work options. He was absolutely adamant. He said he had to function twenty-four hours a day and that this required three eight-hour shifts. A peer asked him why he couldn't do six four-hour shifts. He looked at him, speechless. And came up hours later to admit that it was a legitimate question and that it had never crossed his mind. Our existing patterns are deep, and we take them as inalterable. Until we alter them.

FRONTLINE FEEDBACK: *"We count part-time employees as FTEs. Managers don't have much incentive to hire people into part-time roles. This is a US-centric thing – something to do with how the Street calculates headcount."*

Dual careers and international mobility are the other big issues perceived to influence gender balance. They are seen more as issues for women, although more and more men are affected as well. In "hot" emerging markets, top talent is less mobile because there are so many good opportunities locally, and family pressures are often stronger than in many Western countries. The more that mobility is linked to identifying and developing high-potentials, especially when workers are in their thirties, the more women, as mothers, and some men, as fathers, fall off that list. Without a proactive eye toward gender balance, women fall out of the high-potential pipeline – and never make it back in. This often happens unconsciously and not as an official policy or known obstacle; it is simply a systemic disappearance of talent that affects one gender more than the other.

The gender bilingual approach creates working styles that are flexible for everyone.

Give Parental Leave

Companies are not yet very bilingual on the issue of parental leave, a key component of retention gaps between the sexes in many countries. A few firms have managed to allow more flexibility for women to be mothers without derailing their careers, but far fewer have adapted to encourage men to be fathers. This is a double standard, in which companies accept women's family priorities but expect men to always put career and company first. Again, the voices of real executives reveal how much still needs to change:

- "There is no way I could have gotten to where I have today without the support of my (stay-at-home) wife. Each time we moved, she allowed us to start over from scratch with network, friends, schools and all of the other tremendously challenging things. It's a one earner model. If my wife had continued her career, I could never have had the career I've had. I'm absolutely certain of that."
- "If women take time out of their career for children, it really has an impact on a woman's career momentum. It's really hard for women to restart their career after a break."
- "For five years, we have given some flexibility to mothers; we are miles away from giving it for fathers."

A more gender balanced approach would be to allow both men and women to integrate a healthy self-centeredness around their career ambitions and their commitments to others, starting at home with their own families. At work, this will require leaders to be much more gender neutral around the whole issue of families and much more inclusive of men.

Be Bilingual about Power, Ambition, and Promotion

Today, talent identification and promotion policies tend to favour male models of leadership. Strong service to the system, a self-centred ability to market oneself effectively, a track record in incremental improvements to core products or services, an aura of expertise and skill in impressing others with a great deal of self-confidence – all of these contribute to the expectation that leaders will be powerful self-promoters, able to impress others with their ambition and vision. I always ask companies if displaying ambition is an important component of being identified as high potential. The answer is almost always a resounding yes.

FRONTLINE FEEDBACK: *"Over the past several years, we've lost a lot of senior women. They were squeezed out by men, and maybe weren't as extroverted in their leadership style as their male colleagues expected them to be. Do we really understand and appreciate that women's leadership styles can be different? None of them left to stay home with families; they all left to go to other companies."*

Women, by contrast, tend to display a different roster of attitudes toward power and ambition. They frame their ambitions in terms of serving their team or their customers more than corporate systems. They are socialized to be other-focused in their style and are therefore unlikely to try and push themselves forward. They are much more likely to prefer a collective, collaborative approach. They don't seek to impress with their expertise but are more interested in finding and sharing commonalities. Women think that their results and people skills will speak for themselves. They don't buy into the need to sell themselves in order to be promoted – in fact, they often vociferously reject it. Most companies have not integrated the very different preferences of women into their talent identification systems. Many coaching, mentoring and leadership programs are still aimed at getting women to adopt masculine styles of leadership. And when they do, they are met with dismay – by their male colleagues and by the next generation of women, who are disappointed to see their "mentors" selling out.

The fact that women don't display their ambition leads managers to conclude that women don't want power. This inevitably leads to a group of men asking "What do women want?" and concluding that power and promotion are not on the list. The problem is that this may not be the right question. The real question should be, "What do companies need?" And if leaders believe that gender balance is a business imperative, their job–and their responsibility to shareholders–is to systemically enable it. That may involve a different approach: one where leaders "pull" women into power.

In the twenty-first century, the ability to pull women into leadership will be essential. Leaders can be evaluated and rewarded based on their ability to build balanced leadership teams. Understanding what it takes to attract, retain and develop female as well as male leaders will require a sophisticated level of gender bilingualism. It will also require an acknowledgment that women may not push for power, but that fact may actually make them well-suited to exercising it. Conversely, some men who push for power may not be the most effective choice for a particular role and the times. Whoever proved that ambition was an effective criteria for leadership? To the contrary, many, like Tomas Chamorro-Premuzic, professor of business psychology at University College in London, suggest that the contrary is true. "The main reason for the uneven management sex ratio," he writes on hbr.org, "is our inability to discern between confidence and competence. That is, because we (people in general) commonly misinterpret displays of confidence as a sign of competence, we are fooled into believing that men are better leaders than women."[1] Does any of this sound familiar? It did to many of the male executives I spoke with.

- "We used to have more senior women, but there are fewer now. But the truth is that I am more feminine than many of the senior women who have succeeded here."
- "We had done an external assessment of potential, and all the men who had been judged ready for promotion weren't and all the women who had been judged not ready were. We don't have objective criteria for evaluating readiness. Is it biased? Something is happening in the way we are developing women."
- "It turns out that the culture just didn't work for them. We need to learn to be more attractive as an employer."
- "We have double the percentage of women in our poorest performers. Why? The 'war-room and bring in our top guns' approach and verbiage is a factor. I do think there is a systemic and innate bias in how we look at females."
- "We really need to change our culture. We need to push women into more senior positions and provide (the right) role models. We need to more proactively manage the female talent pipeline."

1. Tomas Chamorro-Premuzic, "Why Do So Many Incompetent Men Become Leaders?," HBR Blog Network, August 22, 2013, http://blogs.hbr.org/2013/08/why-do so-many-incompetent-men/.

Gender bilingual promotion adapts leadership criteria to integrate feminine as well as masculine characteristics. It also trains talent assessors to be more "consciously competent" and familiar with gender differences rather than "unconsciously incompetent," insisting that gender has no significance or impact, while applying an unconscious preference for masculine behaviours.

Companies that align their systems with their goals find that management behaviours follow. Changing the rules of the game is most clearly spelled out and visible in what employees see other people actually doing – especially their leaders. Shifting your talent management approach from trying to make female managers adapt to creating managers who are skilled in managing across genders will open up a wellspring of underexploited talent, ideas and innovation.

And what is true on the talent side is even more true on the market side.

8. Gender Bilingual Marketing

Companies' mission statements are often a good indicator of their gender bilingual abilities. Here again, do machines or people dominate? Does the organization lean toward a self-serving enhancement tool to improve a buyer's competitive position and performance, or a more utopian, "other-focused" goal to save the world or some part of it? While mission statements have traditionally been an internally focused message, they have moved over into the marketing domain. And with good reason. Customers, shareholders and a broad swath of stakeholders increasingly care about what a company thinks it does. From Google's (in)famous "Don't be evil" statement to IBM's "Solutions for a smarter planet" tagline, the mission is increasingly the message.

Gender bilingual CEOs tend to underline the broad scope of their companies' responsibilities, embracing the other-focused dimensions. So Ursula Burns, chairman and CEO of Xerox and also the first black woman to lead a Fortune 500 company, has been widely praised for saying, "We all need to be more impatient with the status quo. I believe we all need to shift the emphasis in our thinking – from why we can't create more jobs to how we can create more jobs . . . from why we can't compete to how we can compete . . . from why hunger and poverty and injustice exist in the world to how they can be eliminated." Or Jayne-Anne Gadhia, the newly appointed CEO of Virgin Money, who makes it her mission to save us all from the banking sector. She has said: "We've made no secret of our ambition to build a new kind of bank in the UK, one that makes everyone better off – customers, staff, shareholders, partners, and the communities we serve. We're here to build a bank that's fair, transparent and honest."

FRONTLINE FEEDBACK: *"We do a terrible job of understanding the female consumer. We are a company that runs on facts and figures, not on emotions."*

Gender bilingual mission statements build bridges by going beyond performance and competitive edge to acknowledging and addressing a company's role in the world, and its legacy for future generations.

Who Is Your Customer Becoming?

In industries from telecoms to law firms to manufacturing, I've heard a variety of objections to looking at customers through the lens of gender.

- There's no difference between male and female customers.
- It's a sub-issue; it's not important enough to make a difference to the bottom line.
- We have no female customers.

- Our salesforce needs to be male because men prefer buying from other men.

As they start to get over these assumptions, the first step of many male-dominated companies when trying to integrate female customers is to add a tentative little test. They develop a niche product, aimed specifically at women. You see a lot of this in the financial sector now, with services aimed at women. These can be lucrative niches, but in no way do they match the potential of actually doubling the size of your market by making products that appeal equally to both genders. Keeping your blinders on is a great way to keep your profits small.

Smartphones, for example, used to be considered an entirely male segment, aimed at executives with the need for power in their pockets. They were complicated devices with lots of sophisticated software and accessories. My clients at the time assured me that their market research showed that women weren't interested. They had very sophisticated market segmentation showing life stages and economic profiles and buying habits. Gender was included in the mix, but it was buried deep within it. It had never been pulled out and tested first, to see if there were any tangible, usable differences between male and female customers or between male and female noncustomers.

FRONTLINE FEEDBACK: *"When we talk about our consumers and shoppers, we always refer to how 'she' would do this or that. Yet, there are no women sitting around the top table."*

Then Apple joined the fray. Unlike most of its competitors, Apple did not settle for developing a pink, flowered phone for the ladies (as Siemens did with the CL75 flip phone – which they sold with the tagline, "Most phones are from Mars. This one

LETTING WOMEN RUN A MARKETING CAMPAIGN AIMED AT WOMEN? IT'S NOT ONLY UNFAIR BUSINESS PRACTICE — IT'S TOTALLY SEXIST
ROGER BEALE

is from Venus"). Instead, it put gender bilingualism at the heart of its product – not to mention its entire sales and marketing strategy. How to appeal and respond to both male and female needs, without turning off one or the other? Apple discovered what many innovators have found: if you meet women's buying expectations, you exceed men's. So Apple integrated women's preferred product features: namely, beauty and simplicity. Design became a respected, central dimension of the product, rather than an afterthought or a frill. Apple stores look more like luxury fashion emporiums than any of its competitors' electronics retailing outlets, staffed with a gender balanced sales team selected as much for their interpersonal skills as for their technical chops. Within eighteen months of its launch, Apple had a gender balanced customer base for an expensive smartphone product that had long been unquestioningly assumed to be male dominated. In so doing, it also exploded the potential size of the market well beyond its traditional customer base.

FRONTLINE FEEDBACK: *"There is groupthink when any gender dominates. There is a real opportunity to develop far more sophisticated and responsive products, but senior levels are all white, middle-aged males; this is still the default mode."*

Some sectors are flipping the other way. Companies in traditionally female categories are discovering the growing potential of the male market and increasingly developing products aimed at men. For instance, the Mini Cooper was originally positioned as a car for women, and BMW has since done a lot of work to "masculinize" the brand. Unilever has grown their personal grooming business by adding lines targeted aggressively at men, such as Axe. Before assuming that your customer base is exclusively male or female, do some research and carry out focus groups. The world is changing fast. More important, are women or men a huge potential new market? Have you sized it correctly and are you responding to it fully?

Take a Gender Bilingual Look at R&D and Innovation

Companies can revolutionize sectors by integrating women's preferences into its definition of innovation. An increased focus on customer relationships and services rather than on products themselves would be a revolution in itself in many sectors. For example, while parts of the automotive sector have worked to integrate women's needs into its cars, they have not been able to adapt their sales and service networks away from male-dominated car showrooms. Yet this remains one of women's greatest dissatisfactions with the sector and leads to specialized websites that compensate for the fact that women hesitate to enter showrooms.

FRONTLINE FEEDBACK: *"I have learned that when it comes to customers, it's important to think carefully about the match between our team and the customer. In the past, we focused on selecting people with good product knowledge. But actually we need to be thinking about what type of person would be the best fit for a customer relationship in terms of gender and culture? This actually requires more thought than I had put in before."*

Harley-Davidson is one case study that Jane Cunningham and Philippa Roberts describe in *The Daring Book for Boys in Business*. CEO James Ziemer realized that "fifty percent of the population is female and there is pent-up demand. We need to remove the barriers." He did not benchmark the competition or try to focus R&D on a bigger, better, faster motor for his existing line of motorcycles. Instead, he realized that the real innovation would be to redefine his customer segment and open it to the other half of the population. An entire sales and marketing strategy aimed at women was the result, complete with a tagline that touted, "Your life. Your voice. Your ride." The company launched a website aimed at women, catering to their lack of familiarity with motorcycles. Says Ziemer: "The goal is to unambiguously give women the confidence to enjoy the category."

For many companies, redefining innovation away from the machine and toward better understanding of today's noncustomers would dependably open up enormous market potential.

FRONTLINE FEEDBACK: *"A lot of people here are geeks, science and tech-driven people. They think in terms of product features. But it's increasingly clear that the soft part of the design, and what it adds to the customer's personality, is what we need to focus on. In this we are blindfolded."*

Gender bilingual innovation goes beyond only improving the product and technology. It also redefines the market, services, or channel strategies. It has a broader definition of innovation that goes beyond the machine and into customers' hearts and minds.

Rethink Customer Relationships

So many sectors still prefer what Cunningham and Roberts call the "expert sales representative," as opposed to the girlfriend approach preferred by women. From cars and electronics to the medical and financial sectors, experts proliferate, trained to expose their knowledge to customers in order to impress them into buying. This often leads to a lot of expertise on display, complete with the coded language much beloved by experts in any field to signal that they belong.

The girlfriend approach works to erase these differences and put everyone at ease. It strives to create relationships of trust and similarity. The goal is for salespeople to mirror their customers' realities and concerns because they share them, rather than attempting to impress them with their greater knowledge.

The language of complexity rife in any number of sectors is so common it is not even seen as an issue in most companies. The phone operators' pricing policies, the financial sector's product descriptors, the legal profession's language in general, the automotive sector's love of numbers and technical performance criteria, the high tech sector's bits and bytes. All are meant to impress. Women's dissatisfaction with these sectors is high and offers an opportunity for huge business growth.

> **FRONTLINE FEEDBACK:** *"Eighty percent of our customers are women. Naively as an industry we haven't utilized that inherent insight in terms of our proposition, store design, product offering."*

Offering customer relationships with salespeople who understand women's preferences would be a radical innovation in many sectors.

DIY stores have done this rather well in a number of countries. Stores that used to be dark and crowded "man caves" full of an incomprehensible range of tools have often been transformed into IKEA-like displays of design transformation, complete with educational hubs, gender balanced staffs, and lighter, smaller tools adapted to women.

The banking sector, due for a reputational makeover, is venturing in this direction. Virgin Money's Gadhia is trying to transform retail banks into informal, female-friendly salons, ripe for a confidential conversation between equals. The bank's retail outlets are chic living rooms with open desks and a lot of design, a million miles from the traditional separation between "expert" and banking client.

As she told the *Times of London*, "banks must be more transparent and customer focused, two qualities the banking industry has struggled to embrace . . . After the financial crisis, consumers expect their banks to have a real set of values. The majority of customers say that banks 'have responsibility to help people thrive' and 'to help educate people on financial matters."

While "customer centricity" is a buzzword in most companies, the feminine understanding of the term and its application are quite different from the masculine. And it is helpful to keep both perspectives in mind when analysing what customers and end users want. Many companies in male categories don't even integrate a gender dimension into their analyses of their customer satisfaction or expectations, considering it irrelevant – until one of their competitors proves it isn't.

FRONTLINE FEEDBACK: *"I took a different approach from my male colleagues in selling beer. I understood that women buy a lot of the beer, and they want information about the beer to help them make their purchasing decision. My approach sold more than my male colleagues."*

The online world is mirroring the offline world, with a wealth of additional data on consumer behaviour and preferences. Google has shown that men and women use different search words, use different sites, and dominate many of the social networks differently. Being in "girlfriend" mode dictates a close and responsive relationship with customers. And yet traditional corporate approaches can get in the way. For instance, the legal department of one client company had barred all employees from direct interaction on social media sites with clients.

What kind of services do companies offer on their websites? Simplicity, aesthetics, humans to speak with? Or complicated, expertise-laden technicalities? A focus on products, their characteristics, and their superiority to the competition? Or a focus on people, their lives, and needs at different life stages and circumstances?

Gender bilingual customer relationships combine excellent products with outstanding customer connections. They don't focus entirely on one or the other but cover both, usually delighting not only women but men as well.

What Are Your Communications Communicating?

A review of websites and advertising will tell you all you need to know about the degree of gender bilingualism in companies. One of the challenges on the advertising front is that the vast majority of creative directors in advertising firms (90 percent) are men. They have unconsciously imbued traditional masculine values into a majority of advertising that then does not speak to women. So it may actually take some strenuous briefing of your advertising teams to get them even to understand what you are trying to do. This may be harder in certain countries where gender stereotypes are strong.

A look at either end of the spectrum can be useful in calibrating some middle ground. For instance, advertising for Red Bull is about pushing yourself to extremes – the highest peaks, the coldest mountains, the farthest gorge. It is heroism come to life. Compare this to department store John Lewis's ad that celebrates all the phases of a woman's life, integrating life, work, children, grandchildren, love, and relationships. It's like a different planet.

Is there a way for advertising to integrate both male and female preferences?

Very few companies have even consciously tried to be more gender balanced. Some exceptions are new, younger companies, including Apple, Google, and Nike, which consider their products to be gender bilingual and enjoy mass, gender balanced appeal. Their advertising and communications involve trying to find what men and women share, in a way that acknowledges the differences and then finds ways of addressing both through the same channels. They tend to dig into the deeper, underlying human values. They focus on finding what men and women share: values, life, love, family, connection.

Gender bilingual sales and marketing approaches cover the full life cycle of customers and the entire range of company activities from R&D and development to distribution and after-sales service strategies, online and off. Execution is obviously affected by the gender balance of the sales and marketing teams in-house. Be careful, though: The solution is not, as I have seen in many companies, to have marketing staffs dominated by women. The idea is to carefully think through who your customers are today, where the biggest potential new customer growth will be tomorrow, and how much a strategic use of gender differences and balance can contribute to business growth.

CONCLUSION

Globally, women in nearly every country are earning higher-income jobs and roles – socially, economically, and politically. They are now the majority of the educated talent in many of the countries on the planet. Global female income now represents more than the combined GDP of China and India – and emerging-market GDP has just exceeded that of the developed world for the first time. Wherever the middle classes rise, the purchasing power of women rises in direct correlation. Are your sales and marketing teams fully embracing the potential of a gender-bilingual approach to global markets? That's where tomorrow's profits lie, and today's smart innovators know it.

FRONTLINE FEEDBACK: *"I am very proud to be working for a company that is concerned with this kind of topic. Maybe we should have done it before, but we are doing it now, and doing it right. In three years, this company will look very different on gender balance. And we will show better P&L, our numbers will be better, and more women will want to work for us. It's a virtuous circle."*

Much of the concern regarding gender issues has been its misframing and the underestimation of its potential impact on business. Or the persistence of twentieth-century frameworks that were once necessary but are now obsolete given current realities. The big change, which I've highlighted in this book, is that smart leaders are now recognizing and repositioning the topic to maximize its strategic impact. Once they do, there is a period of change management required to get managers to understand why gender balance is being newly positioned and pushed. Underlying it all is a need for greater acceptance and understanding of the differences between genders. Successful companies and managers of tomorrow will be global, cross-culturally at ease, and fully gender bilingual. They are even likely, like the ladies getting on their new Harley-Davidsons, to enjoy the ride.

ABOUT THE AUTHOR

Avivah Wittenberg-Cox is the CEO of 20-first, one of the world's leading gender consultancies. 20-first works with progressive companies interested in diversifying their leadership teams and optimizing both halves of the talent pool and both halves of the market – the female and male halves. 20-first works with CEOs, executive committees, and managers to build gender bilingual organizations.

Avivah Wittenberg-Cox is the author of two best-selling books: *How Women Mean Business: A Step-by-Step Guide to Profiting from Gender Balanced Business* (Wiley, 2010); and *Why Women Mean Business: Understanding the Emergence of Our Next Economic Revolution* (Wiley, 2008). *Why Women Mean Business* was awarded the Manpower Best Book of the Year prize in 2009 and was selected as a business book of the year by the Conference Board Review.

Wittenberg-Cox speaks on leadership, marketing, and talent management issues across the globe and has lectured at both INSEAD and HEC business schools. She blogs for *Harvard Business Review* and is the first female columnist for *Der Spiegel's Manager* magazine.

Wittenberg-Cox is the Founder and Honorary President of the European Professional Women's Network and has been recognized by *Elle* magazine as one of the Top 40 Women Leading Change.

Connect with Avivah Wittenberg-Cox on Twitter at @A_WittenbergCox or via email at queries@20-first.com.